God's Li'l People
and Angels

True Stories About Little People
by Mama G.

Illustrations by Young Artists:
Cover:	Shaylah Grech
Grace:	Ericca Arroyo
K. C., Christopher & Gabby:	Nikki Deschambault
Annie:	Jordie Dyck
Alan:	Janae Dyck
Kiley:	James Swartzendruber
Angela:	Hope Pigott
Katrielle:	Katrielle Bauknight
Niki:	Renee Saraco
Kenny:	Mark Dombowsky
Extra Angels:	Granddaughters-Rachel, Annika Arienne, Katrielle

Layout and Design..............Diane Connis

Publisher……….................…Five Stones Publishing
www.ilncenter.com
An International localization Network Ministry
Randy2905@gmail.com

ISBN: 978-1935018-60-5

Dedicated to our Dear Heavenly Papa who deeply loves ALL His little people everywhere

Introduction

This book gives a peek at angels all around us! What an adventure to gather and share these stories, for little people to know their Loving Father—who is always near and can do anything!

The theme of this series was sung years ago by my four little girls. Now is the time for this explosion of God's power in and through the little people!

We are God's little people.
We got a light, and we're gonna let it shine!
We are God's little people.
God's little people are
God's BIG PEOPLE sometimes!

Bold print tells the story to little people, with added details for bigger people.

 Look for the dove in the pictures, a symbol of our Loving Father who is always there. ~ Mama G

Angels

God made angels, millions and millions of them. They help God and they make beautiful music in heaven. God sends them all over the earth, wherever somebody needs help. Some stay with us, our own special helpers.

Some are messengers that bring special messages from God. Some are warriors that fight against the bad angels that try to hurt us.

Some are really BIG. Some are really small. Some work alone. Some are on a team. Some are with thousands of others in an army.

Angels have many, many different jobs to do. They love to help, and they laugh and sing while they work.

Sometimes we can see angels. Alex, (a boy who went to heaven), says the only way to describe angels of all different kinds is: MAGNIFICENT! AWESOME! INCREDIBLE! We learn about angels from the Bible, and from lots of people who have seen them. I hope you will see them too.

You will like these true angel stories. And if you have an angel story we want to hear it too. Every story is special because little people and angels are special to God!

Grace

A baby was born too soon. The doctors said, "She won't live. She is dying!"

She was very tiny, and she was gasping for breath.

Her Mama stayed close by her, crying and praying. Then, on the tenth day, a miracle happened! "My baby is healed," cried Mama.

So she wrapped her up, and hugged her tightly, and took her home. They named her Grace, which means, 'God does what we cannot do!'

When Baby Grace was at home, asleep in her little crib, Mama saw an angel touching her. Then she knew, for sure, that God was taking care of her baby.

As Grace grew up she began to sing and play heavenly music. Maybe you will hear Grace Williams' music someday!

K.C.

K.C. was only four, and she had to stay in the hospital ALL BY HERSELF!

When Mommy came she said, "Oh Honey, I am so sorry I had to leave you last night! I had to go home to the other kids. Did you cry?"

"It's OK, Mommy. A nice man stayed with me all the time," said K.C.

"What man?" asked Mommy.
"Only your daddy visited you."

"He was a big beautiful man with wings!"

"What did he say?" asked Mommy.

"He just stood by the window and watched me. He was so-o-o beautiful!"

And, of course, K.C. got all better again.

Christopher

"Look! Mom and Dad!" said Christopher, who was seven. "Do you see the beautiful angel?"

"She looks bright and gold with sparkles all around her!"

Christopher was in the hospital.
He was very, very sick.

For a long time the doctor was trying to make him well.
But it was not working.

So God sent an angel to help him.
Then Christopher got better really quick!

His infection went away, and he got strong again.
He wanted to go outside and run.
He was so-o-o excited to go home!

But he never forgot the beautiful angel.

Gabby

"Mommy, don't leave me!" said Gabby, as Mommy kissed her and tucked her into bed.

It was a cold winter night in Canada, and three year old Gabby was snuggled under the covers.

"I'm sorry! But I'll be back soon," said Mommy, as she hurried to help the other children.

But when Mommy came back, Gabby was fast asleep.

The next morning, Gabby said, "Mommy, last night an angel sat on my bed and rubbed my back. It was so-o-o nice!"

That made Mommy very, very happy. She smiled at God. He is always watching and knows just what little people need.

Annie

Baby Annie was three months old. But, something was wrong with her little heart!

Mommy was very worried, and prayed for her baby to be well.

Very, very early one morning, big sister Claire (who was three), called,

"Mommy! Mommy! Come quick! See the angels with Baby!"

Mommy couldn't see them, but she knew little Claire did.

After that, Mommy didn't worry anymore. And, guess what?
Baby Annie's heart soon got all better.

Alan

Alan was walking his bike across the street and he did not see the car.
"Beep! Beep! Crash!"
Suddenly, he was flying through the air!

Kind people rushed him to the hospital.

"But I'm fine! Really! I'm OK!"
Alan told the doctor.
"It was like a hand grabbed my shirt and let me down easy!"

Alan had scraped his knee, but it did not hurt much at all, so the doctor let him go home.

His teacher said, "Alan fell rather slowly to the street. It was most unusual! It seemed like an angel was carrying him!"

And for sure it was. You can read about it in the Bible, in Psalm 91.

Kiley

Kiley was twelve when she got pneumonia. She was VERY sick.

Day after day, her mom walked alone in the hospital halls, praying that Kiley would live.

One day she heard a glorious voice in the hallway, singing, "You'll never walk alone. . . ."

A happy man was singing so loud the walls were shaking!

When Kiley's mom ran to see who it was, the man smiled and disappeared! And Kiley was soon all better!

Then Mommy knew the singing man was an angel, and she never felt alone again.

Angela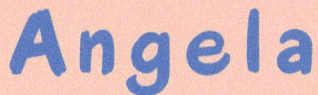

Angela's favorite story about angels happened when she was only two. She was in the hospital for a long time.

Then, she fell into a deep, dark sleep, and she could not wake up.

One night, Daddy was praying by Angela's hospital bed. He was looking up at stars painted on the ceiling.

Suddenly he saw a ladder of light coming down from Heaven. Hundreds of tiny angels were coming down to Angela.

Daddy said, "Oh no! Are you coming to take her away?" But, quick as a wink they were gone. And Angela got all better!

Then Daddy knew that God had sent the angels to help his baby get well.

Katrielle

Katrielle was seven. She liked to get up early. One morning her Daddy whispered, "Kat, do you want to go out for breakfast?"

"Oh, yes!" Kat's breakfast was too big. So on the way home, they stopped to give it to a homeless man. But he did not want it!

When Daddy came back to the car, Katrielle said, "Why didn't you give it to the other one?"

Daddy said, "I don't see anyone else. There is only one person there.

"No," said Kat, "There is a girl laying right there on a bag."

But Daddy could not see her. He said, "You must be seeing an angel!" Kat was very surprised! Do angels sometimes look like people?

Niki

It was summertime in Florida,
and Niki loved playing outside.

The beautiful rain tree in the front yard was covered with flowers.
She could see it from her bedroom window.

"Come here, Kitty, Kitty! Where are you, Punkin?"

When Niki turned five, she
got Punkin for her birthday.

Niki usually played alone, because her sisters
were much older. But she knew she was not alone.
Her Papa God was always with her.

"Oh well, I'll just climb
my favorite, best tree
and listen to the birds."

It was such a nice place to hide,
to listen and to sing to God.

Mommy! Mommy! I fell down! Come quick! The tree broke!

Sure enough! There was the big branch on the ground that Niki had been lying on. But Niki was smiling, She was not hurt at all!

"I'm fine!" said Niki. "I just sort of floated like an angel!" Mommy and Daddy were very surprised. They said, "Niki, that must have been your guardian angel, carrying you down!"

Niki is big now. But she has never forgotten how that felt. Everytime Niki thinks about how God protected her, she smiles. "Thank you, God, for loving me so much!"

Kenny lived in America in a happy little family.

His mommy and daddy played music for opera in New York.
One day, they moved to a little town. They did not have much money.
But they had each other and they had music.

Kenny liked summertime—playing with
his friends, running barefoot, climbing trees,
and swimming in the creek.

One day, Kenny went out to the woods all by himself.

It was 1924, and he was 11 years old. This day he had a special idea in his mind. It was not fishing. It was not swimming.

He was looking for moss that hangs in trees.

It was for his Auntie for her flowerpots and decorations.

Suddenly the branches caught him!
"O-o-o-o-oh! Ouch!"

He stretched and wiggled and twisted,
but he could not get loose.

"Oh dear! Will daddy ever find me way out here?"
Will I have to stay out here all night?

"H-E-L-P!" he cried.
"I need help!" And, then, quietly,
"Can you help me, Dear God?"

Nobody was walking on the path nearby.

Everything was quiet, except for a little bird.

Then suddenly a big man was standing under the tree, looking up at Kenny.

He wore overalls, and an engineer cap. Where did he come from?!

"Can I help you?" asked the kind man.
"Yes, Sir. I'm stuck!" said Kenny.

Big, strong arms lifted Kenny down.

Kenny was so happy to feel his toes on the ground again!
He would not have to stay in the tree all night, with the bugs and the snakes!

He was so happy to be safe at home.
He gave Mommy a big hug.

His daddy did not know who the big man was.
Only God knew. And He did not tell. It was a secret.

Kenny went to bed that night with a happy heart.

Maybe God was giving him a big hug
and whispering a secret in his ear.

But Kenny did not hear.

He snuggled under the covers,
and fell fast asleep.

When Ken was a grampa, his wife got very, very sick. At the hospital, someone sat down beside Ken. "God loves you, Kenny," he said.

Can you guess who it was?

Ken finally knew the secret! The man was an angel!
He looked exactly the same as many years ago in the woods.
He had been Kenny's special helper ever since Kenny was very little.

Ken wiped away his tears when
he saw his angel friend.
God was happy as He watched
them sitting together.

Do you know the secret? *We all have angel friends to help us!*
They help us even when we can't see them.
But now and then, when you least expect it, you just might see them!
Thank you, Papa God!

Watch For New Titles Of God's Li'l People

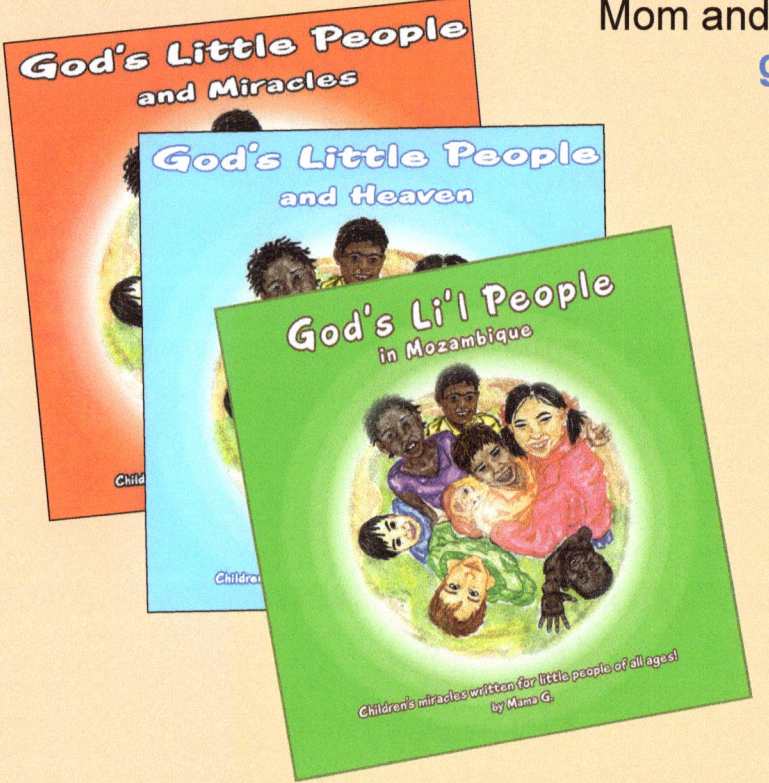

Mom and Dad, check out our website:
godslilpeople.com

Find links,
share miracle stories,
order new books.

Find other language
editions as they
become available.

If you have a miracle story
to share, or would like to do
some pictures for a story,
please write
Thelma Goszleth at:

godslilpeople@gmail.com

Mr. Dietze (Kenny) lived for many years with his family in Pennsylvania. He was a wonderful, kind man who always loved God. At 90, he was still playing his trombone and singing.

Ken is now in Heaven, probably enjoying music with his wife and his angel friend!

www.ingramcontent.com/pod-product-compliance
Lightning Source LLC
Chambersburg PA
CBHW041633040426
42446CB00025B/3501